Third Eye Awakening

Clara B. Ellen

CONTENTS

INTRODUCTION

Thank you for buying *Third Eye Awakening: Understanding and Opening the Third Eye* and thank you for doing so. Making the decision to learn more about the third eye and the benefits of using it to its fullest potential is a major step and one that should be applauded.

Unfortunately, when it comes to using your third eye effectively, the first step is also the easiest step which is why the following chapters will discuss everything you need to not only understand the third eye and what it means for you but also how to start working to access it on a regular basis. This starts with a discussion of the basics of the ideas behind the third eye, including its storied history throughout the world and even how it is directly related to the pineal gland. With an understanding of what the third eye is under your belt, you will then be ready learn about the primary type of mindset that you are going to want to work to embody to make actually opening your third eye much easier.

After getting a firm grasp on the proper mindset required for third eye meditation, the next thing you will learn is how you can actually start opening your third eye through various meditative and shamanistic practices. Not every practice will be right for every person which is why there is also a secondary chapter on advanced meditation techniques for those who are looking for something a little more tailored to those who have meditated before. You will also learn what to expect as well as many common mistakes to avoid and several tips to make your third eye meditation success somewhat more assured.

There are plenty of books on this subject on the market, thanks again for choosing this one! Every effort was made to ensure it is full of as much useful information as possible, please enjoy!

1 UNDERSTANDING THE THIRD EYE

I am in touch with my inner guidance.
I listen to my deepest wisdom.
I seek to understand and to learn from my life experiences.
I am wise, intuitive, and connected with my inner guide.
I nurture my spirit.
I listen to the wisdom of elders.
I trust my intuition.
I forgive the past and learn what was there for me to learn.
I forgive myself.

I love and accept myself.
I know that all is well in my world.
I am connected with the wisdom of the universe.
I am open to inspiration and bliss.
My life moves effortlessly.
I am at peace.
I am the source of my truth and my love.
-Unknown

This is the affirmation of the third eye. The third eye is the portal which leads to your soul and transcends you to a higher spiritual consciousness. It is symbolic of a heightened state of awareness and evokes images which have deep meaning and significance to the world around you. When awakened, your third eye may allow you to see visons and auras, gain clairvoyance and see the importance of all life around you. The third eye is within us all, but will only manifest itself with deep spiritual practice and intuitive thinking.

Third Eye Basics

The third eye is the sixth of the seven chakras (also known as Anja or the brow chakra). A chakra transcends the physical body and focuses on the inner energy which connects us with the universe. Chakra means "beyond wisdom," and the third eye chakra evokes lucid dreaming, expanded imagination, clairvoyance and visualization. Being in spiritual alignment with all seven chakras helps you see the bigger picture and opens your soul to every part of life. The seven chakras are:

1. Root chakra- The root chakra represents the foundation of our being. It is located at the base of the spine motivates our survival instinct.
2. Sacral chakra- The sacral chakra assesses and processes change. It is located in the lower abdomen.
3. Solar Plexus chakra- The solar plexus chakra gives us confidence and self-control. It is located in the stomach area.
4. Heart chakra- The heart chakra gives us the capacity to love. It is located above the heart.
5. Throat chakra- The throat chakra allows us to communicate through feelings and truth. It is located in the throat.
6. Third Eye chakra- The third eye chakra opens our mind to the enormity of the universe using intuition and spiritual reflection. It is located between the eyes of the face.

7. Crown chakra- The crown chakra is the highest of all chakras. It assists us in connecting fully with spirituality and providing bliss. It is located at the top of the head.

The third eye is an esoteric symbol originally representative of a higher spiritual power. The third eye chakra provides clarity to our thoughts and puts meaning to intuition. It can be considered as the gateway to higher awareness. It lies within all of us, but needs to be awakened. The third eye is also a sense; it interprets the world around us. It helps us see clearly, supports imagination and sharpens our perceptions. For example, when someone goes "on a hunch," this means they have identified and are acting upon their intuition. But is this a hunch, or a product of third eye awakening? The third eye allows us to see patterns of energy which uncover deeper truths and connects each moment to each other.

The third eye chakra blessing:

May your wisdom serve others. May your insight bring you new levels of spiritual awareness. May you understand your true nature. May you see clearly in every way.

Misinterpretation of the third eye

Modern day understanding of the third eye is not spiritual in nature and may even be considered as malevolent. Talk of a third eye may conjure up an image of the dollar bill, which shows an open eye levitating above a pyramid, surrounded by rays of light. This symbol is called the Eye of Providence, or better interpreted as the all-seeing eye of god. Today in the United States, the Eye of Providence is associated with Freemasonry. Freemasonry is the oldest and largest fraternal organization in the world.

It was founded in 1717 in London to regulate stonemasons and control their interactions with people of authority. Members must believe in a higher power, but it cannot be the Christian interpretation of god or Jesus Christ. In meetings, talk about Christianity or Jesus Christ is banned and the bible is not valued. But neither agnostic nor atheists can join. Freemasons believe in their own savior, and this deity evaluates your life's work and decides if you are going to heaven or hell. Many people see freemasonry as a cult: creating their own higher power, denying certain religions and banning free speech or original thought.

Some modern-day theorists believe the third eye is associated with the "Illuminati," which represents control. The Illuminati is a group of elites (business leaders, innovators and world leaders) who is said to control the world to their liking. No one is quite sure if this group exists or if it is an urban legend. Either way, over time, the third eye went from a wondrous spiritual experience to a symbol of sinister power and control. Now we will examine how the third eye has been used in many ancient cultures as a symbol of enlightenment and wisdom.

History of the third eye

Throughout all human history, the third eye represented some level of wisdom, intuition and spiritual awareness. It can be found in almost every religion and indigenous culture. There are many different interpretations of the third eye, but each have a commonality of peace and enlightenment.

India: The third eye was found in Sanskrit text over 3,000 years ago. It represented the highest level of consciousness and spirituality likened to god. The Hindu god Shiva has three eyes; the third eye located in the middle of the forehead. Shiva holds all knowledge and sees the truth in people. The third eye helps rid the world of evil. When opened, the third eye destroys ignorant and malevolent people.

Nepal: Buddha, the founder of Buddhism, is said to possess the Eye of the World. Images of Buddha usually show a dot between the brows of the eyes which represents to the third eye. He is recognized by Buddhists as a divine and enlightened teacher who alleviates suffering and provides insight about the world to its followers.

Middle East/Asia: In the Middle East, the third eye is named Hamsa and is located in the palm of the hand. It provides protection from violence and evil. Middle Easterners believe there is also an eye on the forehead, but this represents immorality and suffering (this is where the term "giving the evil eye" comes from).

Ancient Greece: Orpheus was a prophet in Greek religion who created the *Hymns of Orpheus*: poems which are representative of Greek spirituality. The hymn "To the Sun" describes the role of the third eye in the western world. It speaks about the "eternal eye with broad survey," compares the third eye with the "Father of the ages" representing "immortal love and bearing light." The poem also call the third eye the "great eye of nature and the starry skies" and "the defender of all that is right."

Christianity: The tomb of Jesus, dating back to 1st century AD, has a third eye symbol above the entrance. In Christianity, the third eye is referred to as the "Eye of God" and is a symbol of God's omnipresence and protector of all creation. The following quotes are taken from the Bible:

- "The light of the body is the eye: if therefore thine eye be single, thy whole body shall be full of light." (Jesus in Matthew 6:22)
- "The eyes of the Lord are on the righteous, and his ears are open to their cry;" (Psalms 34:15)
- "The eyes of the Lord are in every place, beholding the evil and the good." (Proverbs 15:3)

Ancient Egypt: Hieroglyphics of the Egyptian god Osiris is always shown with a third eye. The third eye is called the Eye of Ra or the Eye of Horus and is a symbol of healing and restoration. The left eye is the moon, and the right eye is the sun; and the inclusion of the third eye creates a spiritual force which connects directly to Christ. Interestingly, ancient representations of Osiris's third eye looks very similar to the mid-section of the brain where the pineal gland is located. The pineal gland is said to be the modern adaptation of the third eye. Let's take a deeper look at this.

The pineal gland

The pineal gland is a small endocrine gland which produces melatonin. Melatonin is a derivate of serotonin which regulates wake/sleep patterns (circadian rhythm) in reaction to the length of daylight or darkness. This gland can be found in the center of the brain, above the brain stem and in alignment with the spinal cord.

Academics of ancient religions believe the third eye transformed into the pineal gland as humans evolved. Our ancestors believe the third eye deteriorated over time, transforming into the pineal gland. After this change happened, people lost the ability to connect the physical and spiritual worlds and clairvoyance was buried. Today, the third eye can be opened or "awakened," and this book will teach you how to do so.

Interestingly, many researchers of the third eye believe that sodium fluoride is the reason why the pineal gland is no longer effective in balancing the seven chakras. Some have even gone as far to say that the United States government has secretly been increasing the levels of fluoride in drinking water. Let's explain. In the late 1990's, scientist Jennifer Luke conducted the first study to see how the pineal gland is effected by sodium fluoride. Her research discovered that the penial gland is a magnet for fluoride, absorbing more than any other part of the body, including bones.

This may sound beneficial, but the high amounts of fluoride we consume each day result in the calcification of the gland; reducing melatonin production and disconnecting us from spiritual enlightenment. Sodium fluoride can be found in 90% of the U.S. drinking water and cannot be filtered out without a water distiller. Fluoride can also be found in processed foods, sodas, juices, teas and commercially grown produce. Theorists believe sodium fluoride was first added to drinking water during World War II and given to prisoners in concentration camps. This was so the prisoners could not open their third eye, disconnecting them from the god of their understanding.

Regardless of the source, the pineal gland is the modern-day representation of the third eye and can still be awakened with practice and understanding.

Clara B. Ellen

2 FINDING THE PROPER MINDSET

Before you can truly open your third eye, you are going to want to understand the various mindsets that can make opening it much more easily attainable. First and foremost, it is important to keep in mind that opening your third eye isn't something that you can master by only practicing it for a handful of minutes every day, it is more akin to a way of life than that. By actively working to cultivate the type of mindset that makes it easier to understand the enlightenment that is possible you will find that it is easier for your mind to slip into the type of mindset that will have you experiencing real enlightenment sooner than you might expect.

Always be compassionate: Achieving a state where your third eye is open on the regular will naturally start to make you more compassionate to those around you. As such, if you start making it a habit of being more compassionate to those around you, you will find that you are able to find the right type of meditative mindset when you really are looking for it. In order to properly achieve this state, you are going to need to work to actively stay vigilant of the things you see around you while also keeping your thoughts in check against negativity, skills that will help you when it comes to holding back the tide of regular thoughts while you are actively meditating. Once you get in the habit of being compassionate on a regular basis you will want to focus on the feeling you get just after compassion has been shown and work to extend it for as long as possible. That is the feeling you are trying to attain on a regular basis.

Always be cooperative: Regularly opening up your third eye will allow you to understand the things in your life that you can change along with the things that you cannot. It will give you insight into the things that you can change, but it will also make it easier for you to face the things that you cannot change without a thorough resolution that cannot be shaken with any amount of doubt, resignation or fear. This type of mindset can cultivated in your daily life by working as hard as you can to cooperate with the world at large. This means tuning into the natural rhythms that are going on around you and making a concentrated effort to change your actions in accordance with those patterns.

Once you start making an active effort to go with the flow instead of fighting against every little thing you will find that it is much easier to experience the joy that can be found in every single moment. This feeling is not something that happens naturally, it is a conscious choice that you will need to make in order to take your life in a less tense, more smooth sailing direction.

Always be confident: Once you start making choices based on the information that your third eye has provided; you will find that you are naturally more confident in almost every situation. In order to enact this type of mindset you are going to want to try and be confident when it comes to taking steps to make positive changes to your life as a whole. If you remain confident that the work you are dong to improve your ability to meditate will improve over time, then you can be confident enough to let the future take care of itself.

If being truly confident doesn't come naturally to you, then you are going to need to find a way to cultivate this mindset and there is no reason that you will need to worry about doing it on your own. If you are looking for a confidence boost, then seeking out those who are also working to open their third eyes can be a huge help. Not only will these types of groups help you develop the types of life changing positive habits that you are looking to cultivate. What's more, you are also likely to learn plenty of tips and tricks from individuals who have been at the practice far longer than you.

Always be aware of how you are currently doing: While committing to improving your mindset can be easy in the short term, it can be just as difficult in the long term if you don't monitor your progress as you go along. It is important to remember that there is no reason that you have to be completely on track all of the time. Rather, the thing that matters most is being able to ensure that when you do ultimately stray from whatever it is you want to be doing, you have the strength and the courage to get back on the straight and narrow and try again. What's more, you aren't going to want to beat yourself up over the fact that you slipped up now and then, as long as you don't use an individual mistake as license to make several more then you are still moving in the right direction.

If you are looking to more fully understand your current mindset, then you might find it helpful to take stock of your actions throughout the day and simply determine if they are active or if they are passive instead. If the things that you are doing are active then you are working hard to be as invested in the tasks you are doing as possible, greeting each head on. However, if your actions are passive then you will instead always seem to be reacting instead of creating, running 10 minutes late for every appointment and feeling scatterbrained overall. This can help you to stop and take a moment to refocus in order to ensure long term success.

Clara B. Ellen

3 STARTING TO OPEN YOUR THIRD EYE

The journey towards tapping into your third eye is something that takes time, practice and awareness. Patience is key, and you must have clear mind to feel the power of intuition and wisdom. There are different practices used to open the third eye, each connecting your physical body with your mind and soul. Meditating is the most effective way to develop the sixth chakra, and must be done regularly and with consistency. Many people believe that meditating is unhelpful, and this is usually because they lack the discipline and determination needed to transcend the mind.

Meditation techniques

There are endless ways to meditate, and it is much easier to do than expected. Here are two ways you can start meditating effectively to get the most out of your spiritual journey.

Technique #1:

Step One: Find a place which calms you and is free from noise and distraction. Choose a position which is comfortable and can be sustained for a long period of time. Most people sit cross-legged. Close your eyes.

Step Two: In order to center your soul with the universe, you must be acutely aware of the sensations and feelings in your body. Pay close attention to the weight of your legs, torso, arms and head. Try to connect with every sensation in your body to understand its strength and purpose.

Step Three: Being grounded means being present in the moment and not reminiscent of the past or fearful of the future. It means you are connected to your physical body and feel anchored with your emotions. Imagine your legs are tree roots which have grown deep into the core of the earth. Keep picturing your roots growing deeper and deeper, forming an impenetrable link to the universe.

Step Four: You should be in some form of a meditative state by now. Focus on your breath and the beating of your heart. Repeat steps two and three until you feel a sense of connectedness and calm. Serenity is your goal.

Step Five: Now you should be feeling inner peace and calmness. You can only start stimulating your third eye while in this state of stillness. You must identify what your intention is in awakening this chakra. Think clearly and say what comes naturally to you. For example, you could say, "I am awakening my third eye to connect with the patterns of the universe and elevate my spiritual consciousness."

Step Six: Now imagine a lit candle. Look at it slowly and pay attention to each detail. Is the flame flickering? Is the candle tall or short? Is wax dripping? Continue to picture this candle while focusing on your breathing. If you become distracted, visualize yourself pushing the thought out of the way and refocus on the candle.

Technique #2:

Step one: Relax. Try the 4-7-8 breathing exercise. Breathe in through the nose for four seconds. When inhaling, make sure your shoulders do not rise. You want to breathe into your diaphragm instead. Think about inflating your stomach with oxygen. Now hold the breath in for seven seconds (or however long you can handle) then exhale for eight seconds. Repeat until you feel the tension flow away from your body.

Step two: Pray. It does not have to be religious in nature. Ask for your higher self to guide you through this journey.

Step three: Be still. Any movement will send energy to your muscles. You want all your energy to be pushed outwards. Picture yourself as a mountain. You are solid and cannot move.

Step Four: Look up. Even though your eyes are closed, look slightly upwards at a 45-degree angle. This is very important and must be sustained throughout this exercise. Doing this will align your inner vision with your third eye and direct your energy into your spinal cord.

In the beginning, both of these meditation techniques should take around ten minutes, increasing with experience. Try not to pay attention to time, as time does not exist while you are in a deep meditative state. The key to meditation is consistency. Determine what times of the day are best for you and do not stray from this routine. Don't worry if meditation feels uncomfortable at first. Many of us are unable to completely "turn off" and free the mind from all thought. It takes practice, but soon your mind will be free from distraction and closer to awakening your third eye.

Take a shamanic journey

Another way to start tuning into your third eye is by taking a shamanic journey. Shamanism is an ancient spiritual ritual which originated in Siberia and was used in many native cultures. The practice of shamanism guides you into an altered state of consciousness, where you can interact with and gain wisdom from the spiritual world.

The practice of shamanism allows you to take this knowledge and compare it to the patterns of the universe.

There are five aspects which make up shamanism:

1. Shamanism is founded upon the power of Mother Earth. Indigenous people discovered truths and lessons in nature.
2. Shamanism provides health and well-being for those journeying, and provides healing to the entire community; including animals, plants, people and all other forms of life.
3. Engaging in shamanism exponentially grows your spiritual life and creates internal harmony and external peace.
4. Shamans can take energy from the land and honor the natural beauty of scared places like mountains, rivers, lakes and caves.
5. Shamans engage in ritualistic ceremonies to honor the spiritual world and the natural world. Shamanism promises that when these ceremonies occur, the spirits grant the

people with balance and harmony and guarantees the world will continue to exist.

A shamanic journey helps with emotional and physical healing, connects us to nature and aids in personal growth. During the journey, your soul leaves the body and enters the spiritual world where you will receive messages and enlightenment about the world around you. Here is an outline on how you can take a journey of your own:

Preparation: Do not use tobacco products, consume alcohol or take any drug (that is not prescribed to you) twenty-four hours before you start your journey. You do not want the effects of a substance to dull the energy of the journey. If possible, do not eat three hours prior to starting the shamanic journey. It is okay if you do, but a full stomach may block you from having a deep shamanic experience.

Light physical activity, like walking or yoga, is another great precursor to your journey. When we move, our attention shifts into the body and reduces physical and mental tension.

Use a space where you will be free from all external distractions and void of light. Turn off anything that could make noise while you are journeying. You can surround yourself with candles, gifts from nature or other calming pieces.

The journey: To start, sit in a slightly reclined position and relax your muscles. Make sure neither your hands nor legs are crossed. An integral part of a shamanic journey is the sound of repetitive drumming. Drumming is an effective way to be transported into your internal state of consciousness. Shamanic drumming is quick, with six beats per second. You can have someone drum for you or find an audio recording to suit your needs. There are many resources available for those who are serious in taking a shamanic journey.

Focus on the sound of the drums and close your eyes. What do you see? Allow your mind to wander and create pictures in your mind. Try not to suppress anything and just go with the flow of your imagination. Keen in on your senses, both in the physical world and in the spiritual world. Be curious about your inner screen and try to identify any patterns or images. Or you can intentionally focus upon a certain object and imagine it as a portal to the spiritual world. At this point you should in an altered state of consciousness, which will allow you to view life and life's dynamics from a spiritual perspective.

Some of the images presented to you during a shamanic journey are standard for many journeyers. The other images you see are a combination of your imagination and the information the spiritual world wants you to know. This deeper understanding of the universe around us will provide you with insight which cannot be received without being an altered state of consciousness.

If you do not feel comfortable doing this on your own, it is recommended to seek out a shamanic instructor to help guide and support you during your journey. Some journeyers rather be instructed through the process, especially during the first time. Find what works best for you and don't become frustrated if you do not achieve the clarity the journey is supposed to supply.

Five lessons to remember

If you are feeling overwhelmed, lost or discouraged, keep these five lessons in mind to help you release your fears and open your mind and heart. Awakening your third eye is a gift from the spiritual world and achieving this state of being is not a simple task. Repetition, consistency and patience will help you open your soul to the world around you. Remember these five lessons and use them as pointers to keep you centered and grounded.

Lesson one: Slow down. It is very important to pause so you can hear what your soul is trying to tell you. You cannot hear anything if you are blocked by stress or rushing around. Opening the third eye requires patience and grounding. Without pausing and looking at the world around you, you may miss a vision or an opportunity to use your intuitive power.

Lesson two: If you experience a vision, do not freak out. This will take meaning away from what the your subconscious is trying to convey to you. Stay calm.

Lesson three: Practice watching the life around you. Sit on a bench in a busy park or at a shopping mall. Your third eye helps you see patterns of energy, which supports your overall intuition. The longer you are an observer, the easier it will become to see patterns in the world around you to help interpret your third eye experiences.

Lesson four: Pause again.

Lesson five: Learn how to utilize all your senses to properly interpret what your third eye may be telling you. Take time to sharpen your intuition skills by slowing the process down and absorbing everything is around you.

The techniques explained above will help you reach a point of calm and sharpen your intuitions. Remember, the third eye is within us all, we just need to right tools to awaken its power.

Positive Music

Google: Peta Minter Home Studio Melbourn A Shamanic Drum... Great for grounding.

Vagus Nerve, therapy - Calms

Meditation in Rythm.

4 KNOWING WHAT TO EXPECT

By now, you have a good understanding of the third eye and how to open it. This can be an overwhelming experience, especially when you start seeing visions which no one else can see. It is good to know what may happen when you open your third eye so nothing takes you by surprise or frightens you.

How to know if your third eye is open

Some people do not know the exact moment when their third eye was awakened. Just because you do not have visions immediately does not mean your eye is not open. It can be gradual process, so pay attention to how you feel at all times. Here are five signs which will serve as your clues to know when your third eye is open:

1. Opinions are valued: It can be easy to discount someone if their opinion differs from ours. But no one sees the world through the same lenses, and it is important that we keep our minds open to everything we are presented with. If you find yourself judging less and wanting to learn more about people, your third eye may be open.

2. The impossible becomes possible: Before opening you third eye, you had limited awareness and a linear frame of mind. When your sixth chakra has been released, your mind clears and you feel a new level of confidence. Your state of mind changes, and you will be prepared to take on challenges and execute them with ease after your third eye opens.

3. Your senses sharpen and heighten: After you awaken your third eye, all your senses become in-tune with what's around you. You may get a gut feeling that something is wrong or intuitively know something is going to happen before it does. You will see the direction in which energy flows and use this as a guide to find your inner psychic abilities.

4. You become creative: As your awareness for all that is around you increases, so will your appreciation for the beauty and simplicity that life has to offer. You will be presented with images and feelings never seen or felt before, and this new information will unleash your creativity; both in actions and thought.

5. Your relationship with food changes: In ancient cultures, all sources of nourishment were foraged or hunted for. Today, a lot of what people consume contains preservatives or ingredients not found in nature. But along this journey, your body and soul will start yearning for simple and nutritious foods, food that our ancestors ate. Your eating habits are also likely to change as your spiritual self emerges.

What happens once your third eye is open

Once your third eye is awakened, you will start to feel and see the power of this chakra. It is normal to feel overwhelmed or even frightened when you start to have visions and feel things which are out of the ordinary. Here are some things to remember when your third eye is fully awakened so they don't take you by surprise and potentially break your connection with a higher power.

1. Your emotional state matters: Once you are connected to the spiritual world, you may encounter different beings who have insight to share with you. If you are feeling any negative emotions like unease, fear or anger, then your experiences may also be unpleasant. This is because you are emotionally vulnerable to the changes that are happening around you. Your soul must stay balanced and centered in order to absorb the knowledge and power being presented to you. If you are confronted with a spiritual being, keep your mind and soul open, as these beings are reflections of your inner self.

If you are tapped into the spiritual world, you are going to feel a powerful inflow of energy radiating throughout your body. This can be unnerving and uncomfortable at first. If you are starting to feel overwhelmed, take pause and start the 4-7-8 breathing technique and keep doing so until for you feel calm again. Spend time outdoors to connect with nature and reap the benefits of the beauty and calm around you. Also, any type of physical activity balances out the energy that is coursing through you.

2. Extrasensory perception: People who have opened their third eye are granted the gift of psychic capability. Like the

third eye, everyone has psychic abilities, but they
awakened until you are on the right spiritua
Awakening your third eye allows you to communi
both the physical and spiritual realms. Here are th six
psychic gifts which may be bestowed upon you:

i. Clairvoyance (clear vision): A clairvoyant is
someone who receives intuitive information
about the past, present or future in the form
of a person, location, event or object.

ii. Clairaudience (clear hearing): Clairaudience
is the ability to hear sounds which exist only
in a different realm of consciousness.

iii. Clairsentience (clear sensation): This is the
ability to feel and see the feelings and
emotions of people, animals and spirits.

iv. Clairtangency (clear touching): Clairtangency
allows you to feel the touch of a spiritual
entity, which provides you with information
about that being without speech.

v. Clairgustance (clear tasting): This happens
when you can taste something but there is
nothing in your mouth. This allows you to
experience a new taste that is only found in
the spiritual realm.

vi. Clairscent (clear smelling): Clairscent is
when you smell something which is not
there. This is so you can get used to using all

of your senses while tapping into your psychic abilities.

3. Alignment with the universe: Once you achieve peace with your new abilities, the universe will reward you with a new perspective towards life. You will be able to understand the connection between things which surround you. Being in alignment with the universe, your wishes will manifest themselves faster, your thoughts will be more pronounced and you will be able to manipulate your reality.

Dangers associated with opening your third eye

There are many misconceptions regarding the third eye, stories which may scare people away from the third eye's beauty and magic. The reality is that opening your third eye is safe as long as your intentions are pure and free from evil. What you see is a representation of your true self, so some of your encounters will be positive and pleasant, while others may frighten you. But remember, nothing will hurt you. You may have adverse experiences if you suppress negative emotions often. This is because what you see, feel or hear are manifestations of your inner self. With an open third eye, you may experience parts of your personality which have been lost. This is why consistent and meaningful meditation is so important. And, as your intuition develops and strengthens, you will be better at determining what is true and what is false. So stay educated and take this process seriously.

This chapter was rich with information about what you can expect once your third eye is awakened. No one's experience will be the same, so keep an open mind. Trust that what you see around you is spiritual in nature, not evil.

Clara B. Ellen

5 ADVANCED MEDITATION TECHNIQUES

After you have become familiar with the meditation techniques discussed in chapter 2, the next thing that you are going to want to do is take things up a notch by trying the advanced meditation techniques outlined below. Before you get started, a word of caution; while you may feel anxious to get to these advanced techniques as quickly as possible, it is important to not skip to them directly as you will find that you have better results if you have put in the practice with the starter forms of meditation first.

Tataka Meditation

First and foremost, it is important to avoid attempting this type of meditation if you are on a train, bus, plane, boat or anything else that causes your body to be in motion during the act of meditation.

1. Begin by assuming a cross legged lotus position, if this is not a realistic option for you then you may instead either sit comfortably in a chair or on the floor, as long as you keep your spine straight.
2. Next you will want to close your eyes and start taking

several deep breaths. You are going to want to continue inhaling and exhaling fully for three minutes before moving on to the next step.

3. Once you are properly relaxed, the next thing that you will want to do is start to focus on the point that is slightly above the center point of your eyes, while still keeping your eyes closed. Your eyes should be raised upwards about 20 degrees from where they started, again, while still remaining closed.

4. At a pace that is roughly one number per two seconds, start counting backwards from 100. As you do so you will find that your start to experience a strained sensation; what's more, you will likely find that it is pleasurable instead of undesirable. This is what is referred to as the stillness of eyes and it is often associated with an immediate clarity of mind and transparency of thought

5. You will want to continue from 100 all the way to 1, though you should stop if the strain starts to shift away from pleasurable. You should eventually strive to retain this state for two full 100 to 1 cycles. If you find that you are observing things internally during this state, then that is your third eye working properly. Given enough practice at this type of meditation, you will eventually find that the constant stream of thoughts will slow to a crawl, before ideally ceasing entirely.

6. When you reach this state of inner peace, you will want to hold onto it for as long as you can, ideally for upwards of 15 minutes.

7. When it is time for you to end your mediation, you will want to avoid simply snapping back to reality immediately as the difference can be jarring enough to undue much of the work that you have done. To start, you will want to

slowly release your eyes from this position and let them naturally return to a resting state. You will then want to do the same with your consciousness, making a specific effort to disconnect from your third eye and return to the present.

8. Focus on nothing but your breathing for an additional three minutes before opening your eyes and completing your meditation.

Energy Wave Meditation

This type of meditation is all about eliminating distractions as much as possible which means you are going to want to give yourself a minimum of a 30-minute window where you can be reliably free of distractions which means turning off all of your electronic devices, wearing comfortable clothing and the like. Additionally, you might find this type of meditation most effective when you practice it after you have just woken from sleep as the period just after waking is that which is most conducive to meditation.

1. Assume the lotus position or another position that you can sit in comfortably, with your spine straight, for at least 30 minutes if not longer. For this type of meditation, lying down is also acceptable. The cross-legged lotus position is the one that is recommended as it naturally aligns the chakras.

2. After you have assumed the position you are going to want to continue getting into the proper mindset by, one by one, relaxing every single muscle in your body. You are going to start with your feet and work all the way up to your eyes. It is important to visualize this process as you move through the body, and to picture each and every ligament, bone and muscle relaxing as you do so.

3. As you are visually moving through your body you are going to want to take deep, slow, controlled breaths. A nice, slow repetition is what you are looking for, one that you should try and establish naturally so that you don't need to focus on it in order for it to continue for the length of the period of meditation.

4. Throughout this process you are going to want to be on the lookout for a calming wave of energy to build in your body. You are going to want to be on the lookout for its warmth as once you feel it you are going to want to try and kindle it until it becomes a full-on wave. After the energy builds you are going to focus on drawing it towards the center of your forehead where your third eye is located.

5. During this period, it is important to keep your thoughts to a minimum as much as possible as you are striving for a state where none of those cares are currently relevant. It may help to focus on a feeling of weightlessness and to picture yourself getting lighter with every breath as the world around you falls away.

6. At this point you will want to picture a ball of pure white energy rotating at the very center of your mind. Once you can practically touch the ball you are going to want to focus on expanding it slowly and as it does so, let the light of it spill from the point of your third eye. The light is your connection to your third eye and anything you picture in the beam of light that is created will likely be made clear to you regardless of the complicated nature of the topic in question. Repeat the question to yourself until you find whatever it is that you are looking for.

7. When it is time for you to end your mediation, you will want to avoid simply snapping back to reality immediately as the difference can be jarring enough to undue much of

the work that you have done. To start, you will want to slowly release your eyes from this position and let them naturally return to a resting state. You will then want to do the same with your consciousness, making a specific effort to disconnect from your third eye and return to the present.

6 THIRD EYE QUESTIONS AND ANSWERS

Avoiding Third eye obstacles: This enlightened state of mind does not come without moments of frustration and disappointment. This is normal and almost inevitable when you are trying to take on such an enormous undertaking. Here are the top three reasons why people stop third eye meditation:

1. It is not working: Keep in mind this is a lifelong process which will keep developing with time and practice. If awakening your third eye was a simple process, then everybody would be engaging in the practice. Expect some level of results in 2-4 weeks and by 2-4 months your insight and intuition will be developed enough to receive messages from the other world.

2. Postponement: It is human nature to assume something is ineffective if it doesn't produce results right away. Therefore, many people think meditating is useless because they didn't transcend into another realm after their first shot. If you start thinking, "maybe I'll do it tomorrow," this means your intentions are not pure, and you should reevaluate your motivation for awakening your third eye.

3. Your third eye remains closed: One reason why your third eye may not open is because your higher power may not see it fit to do so at the time. Perhaps you are too consumed by stress or work. Remember, patience is imperative, and you never know at what time your third eye will open. It could be ten minutes from now, so don't throw the towel in too prematurely.

Always meditate at the right time: First and foremost, if you plan on getting the most out of meditation right away, then what you are going to want to do is to ensure that you only practice it when you are already in a relaxed state as it will help you to reach the meditative state that you are looking for more easily. As such, it is best to practice in the morning after you have just woken up or after you have just finished up at the gym as opposed to when you have just gotten home from a long day of work and have a million different thoughts all running through your mind at once. If you are hoping to meditate after a stressful day, try taking a short nap beforehand to mellow out and reset your system first.

While this is good advice for novice meditators, eventually you are going to want to try and meditate during as wide a variety of different mindsets as possible, if only to see what the differences are compared to the standard that you have created for yourself. This will help you learn more about your mind, and your third eye will eventually be able to point you towards answers that you would have never come to otherwise.

Avoid fighting to meditate: When you first begin meditating it is important that you do everything in your power to remove yourself from distractions of any shape and size before you get started. While you may eventually be able to meditate while there are other distractions around, for now it is best to either find a distraction free zone or wait and meditate at a later time. The same goes for your mental state, it is more beneficial to wait and meditate later than it is to struggle to calm yourself for 20 minutes or more before you can get anything productive accomplished. After enough practice, you may eventually find that you have something to gain from attempting to meditate while at the same time promoting a mild to moderate amount of physical discomfort. This will allow you to work to hone your meditation and concentration to even greater heights.

Push too hard too soon: When you are first starting out, it is important to not try and break any meditation records and to instead start with short bursts of meditation until you begin to increase your stamina with the practice. When it comes to enhancing your meditation effectiveness, it is important to focus on quality over quantity and ensure that the time you spend meditating is time that you actually spend with a clear mind trying to bring forth the hidden power of your third eye and not simply time you spend sitting in a room with your eyes closed and your legs crossed. You are the only arbiter of your meditation effectiveness, don't shortchange yourself.

The same goes for the amount of effort that you put into meditating on the regular. Meditation shouldn't be something that requires a great deal of effort and should instead be something that comes about from the unified relaxation of mind and body joining together. If you exude too much effort under these circumstances, then instead of actually relaxing you will find yourself adding new levels to your tension instead.

Don't always meditate in the same posture: It is common for many people who meditate regularly to only do so in a sitting position despite the fact that there are several other options when meditating in many instances. While it is not suggested for novices, the fact of the matter is that meditating while walking is actually known to generate a large amount of positive mental energy that is also great for naturally improving concentration. Additionally, you are going to want to get into the habit of trying to meditate in as many different circumstances and scenarios as possible. Meditate with other people, meditate alone, it doesn't matter how you do it, it only matters that you expand your horizons regularly in order to ensure you are always expanding your meditation horizons.

In fact, with enough time and practice you will likely find that you are able to maintain a mild meditative state even when you are otherwise focused on the world around you. This is known as a state of mindfulness and it should be the end goal of everyone who is new to the meditative practice. Being mindful means always being connected to a calming and soothing mental state as well as one that is full of joy and peace which benefits not just yourself but everyone around you.

React appropriately when you find your mind full of thoughts: When you are practicing third eye meditation it is important to not let every single stray thought that floats into your head interrupt your meditative experience. Instead, you may find it helpful to picture all of the thoughts that are passing you by as existing within bubbles that are floating into and out of your field of vision. When a new bubble floats by instead of letting it disrupt your practice, all you need to do is wave it away without letting it disrupt your overall momentum.

Give up without a fight: While it is important to not waste your energy when it comes to meditating when your situation or body simply isn't feeling it, at the same time you are going to want to persevere if at first you don't obviously find a state of meditative bliss right out of the gate. It is important to work at it for a reasonable period of time before chalking it up as a loss and moving on. Only by working at making the early stages easy to power through will you find the long-term success that you seek.

Go into the process in the right way: While there is plenty to be learned from opening your third eye, it is important to only undertake it for the right reasons. As such, if you are looking at to use meditation as an escape from your everyday existence then you are going into the process in a negative way and should consider alternatives that may better help you to address the root cause of your issues. However, if you approach meditation in the right way then you will often find that it can help to improve your life in ways that you would not have previously believed possible.

Spread out the meditative practice: While spending focused bursts of time meditating deeply will provide serious results to your ability to reliably gain insight from your third eye, that doesn't mean it is your only option. Rather, you can work to spread this feeling out continuously by trying to start the day off in the type of mindful mindset that makes interacting with the third eye possible. This means waking up and starting the day in a mindful fashion, and then working to keep it up even when the going gets tough and a myriad of different thoughts are assaulting your ability to keep the right mindset from all sides.

A great time to practice extending this mindset beyond a set period of time is when you are doing household chores. Doing chores provides the right mix of physical exertion and repetition to put the mind in a mindful state practically without trying. Instead of filling this time with music or podcasts, try using it to clear your mind entirely and you will be well on your way to enhancing your ability to interact with your third eye on a constant basis.

7 **CONCLUSION**

Thank for making it through to the end of *Third Eye Awakening: Understanding and Opening the Third Eye*, let's hope it was informative and able to provide you with all of the tools you need to achieve your goals whatever it is that they may be. Just because you've finished this book doesn't mean there is nothing left to learn on the topic, expanding your horizons is the only way to find the mastery you seek.

The next step is to stop reading already and to get ready to get started opening your third eye like you never before thought possible. Before you get started, it is important that you are prepared both emotionally and physically for the myriad of experiences that you have the possibility of tapping into if the third eye opening experience proceeds as planned. This means that for the best results you are going to want to ensure that you go into the experience with the proper mindset, knowing what to expect and how you are going to get the most out of the experience as possible.

First and foremost, however, it is important to never go into the experience expecting something monumental and life changing to happen all at once. An expectant mindset is different than one that is truly clear of all of the types of blockages that can make it difficult to truly tap into your third eye and all of the knowledge that it is waiting to provide. Instead of being expectant, it is more productive to be content with the results of a positive meditative experience and look upon the opening of the third eye as a beautiful bonus rather than the expected end to a mindless ritual. Remember, you are only ever going to get out of the meditative experience what you are capable of putting in. Or, to put it another way, if you can't ask the right questions you will never find the right answers.

Finally, if you found this book useful in anyway, a review on Amazon is always appreciated!

Printed in Great Britain
by Amazon